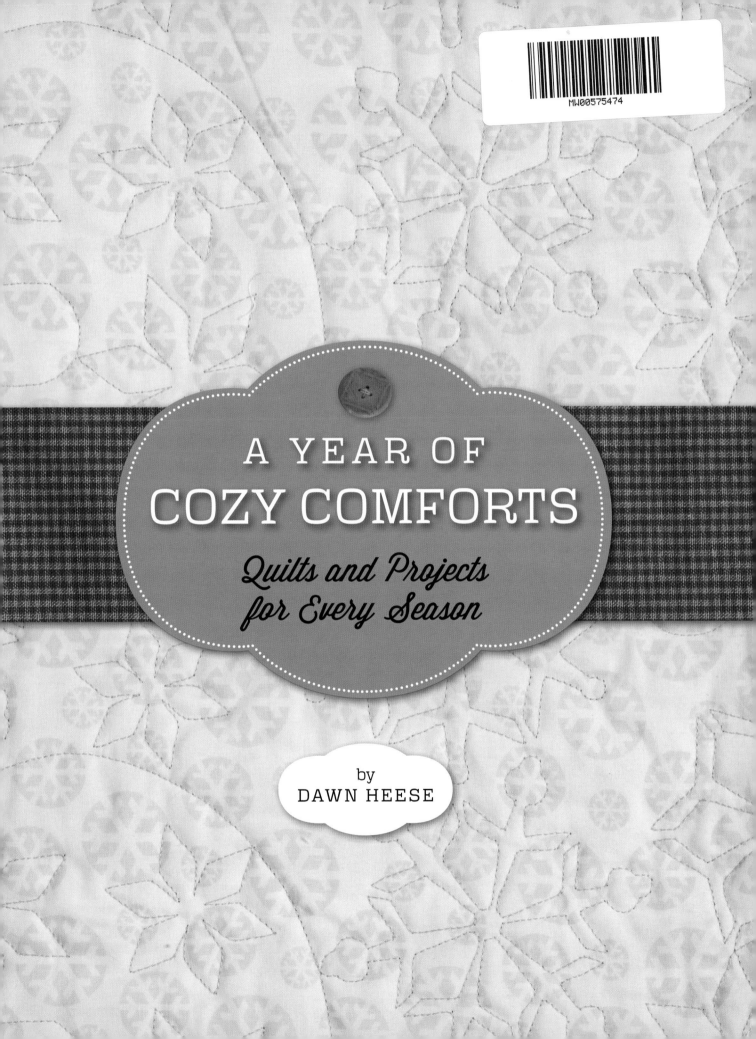

A YEAR OF
COZY COMFORTS

Quilts and Projects
for Every Season

by
DAWN HEESE

A YEAR OF COZY COMFORTS

Quilts and Projects for Every Season

by
DAWN HEESE

Editor: Kimber Mitchell
Designer: Bob Deck
Photography: Aaron T. Leimkuehler
Illustration: Lon Eric Craven
Technical Editor: Nan Doljac
Production assistance: Jo Ann Groves

Published by:
Kansas City Star Books
1729 Grand Blvd.
Kansas City, Missouri, USA 64108

First edition, first printing
ISBN: 978-1-61169-034-7

Library of Congress Control Number: 2011943216

Printed in the United States of America
By Walsworth Publishing Co., Marceline, MO

About the Author

Dawn Heese is a third-generation quilter and an avid cross stitcher. Inspired by a quilt pattern in a magazine, she bought her first rotary cutter and mat in 1999 and hasn't stopped quilting since. She particularly enjoys needleturn appliqué and hand quilting. Her love of traditional designs stems from fond childhood memories of being surrounded by quilts.

Dawn lives in Columbia, Missouri, where she lives with her two teenage sons and works as a hairstylist. She is a member of the Boonslick Trail Quilters Guild as well as several sewing groups. Dawn teaches at quilt shops and guilds nationwide. She has her own pattern company, Linen Closet Designs, and her designs have been featured in national magazines. This is her third book with Kansas City Star Quilts. Follow Dawn's quilting adventures and get free quilt patterns at her blog, dawnheesequilts.blogspot.com.

TABLE OF CONTENTS

Spring

Summer

Fall

Winter

"The seasons are what a symphony ought to be: four perfect movements in harmony with each other."

–Arthur Rubenstein

INTRODUCTION

Here in the Midwest we have four very distinct seasons and each one marks a new beginning. Even though I tend to favor some seasons over others, I still look forward to all of them. The air takes on a new feel, and with it, I find myself changing my indoor environment to match it. I have a closet full of decorative items and quilts that I rotate out to display throughout my home, depending on the time of year. These accents set the mood, while creating a sense of tradition. I love how they make the house look and feel different. Just by changing a few pillows or swapping out a couple quilts, my home takes on a new personality—from cool and casual to warm and cozy.

With each new season, I also find myself changing my cooking choices. I have certain recipes that my family has come to expect each season and I have shared some of our favorites in the chapters that follow.

Throughout this book, you will find quilts, projects, and recipes that speak of each season. Even though I love the individual holidays, they are not holiday-themed. Instead, I wanted to create designs that would carry through each entire season. From umbrellas in spring to pumpkin blossoms in the fall, my projects represent the best of the four seasons. I hope they will inspire you to set a warm and welcoming mood in your home throughout the year.

Happy Quilting,

Dawn

DEDICATION

This book is dedicated to quilters everywhere who have bought my books and patterns, made my quilts their own, and listened to me speak. Without you, I would just be talking to myself.

ACKNOWLEDGMENTS

This is the part where I thank everyone who has worked so hard to make this book possible. Doug Weaver and Diane McLendon are always at the top of that list. They gave me my start as a quilt book author and continue to support me.

A close second is Kimber Mitchell, my editor. Kimber has been with me for all three of my books with the Kansas City Star and without her help and expertise, there would be no books.

Bob Deck for the fabulous design work on this book and the ones that came before.

Aaron T. Leimkuehler, photographer extraordinaire. His photos say it all.

A special thanks to both Bob and Aaron for traipsing around the wet gardens at Shelter Gardens in Columbia, Missouri, where we took the setting shots, to find the best ones for this book. We had to simulate four seasons in just one day!

Lon Eric Craven for his wonderful artwork.

Jo Ann Groves for tweaking the photos to make them just right.

Nan Doljac for her technical expertise in making sure my mathematical calculations were correct.

Tammy Bush of Form and Function Quilting for the beautiful quilting on the April Showers, Pumpkin Blossoms, and Winter Blues quilts.

Weeks Dye Works for the gorgeous hand-dyed floss used in my cross stitch pinkeep.

NEEDLETURN APPLIQUÉ INSTRUCTIONS

There are many ways to appliqué. My way is not the "right way", just the method that works best for me. I love to appliqué by hand but I don't like to spend my time doing prep work. I prefer to get right to the stitching! Since I carry my appliqué with me practically everywhere I go, my method requires very few supplies so I don't have to tote a ton of them along. Here are some needleturn appliqué basics.

1. Trace the template shapes on the dull side of a piece of freezer paper. Do not add a seam allowance to the templates. Cut out on the drawn line. The freezer paper will adhere to the fabric many times. If you need four of the same leaf, for example, you need only cut one paper template and reuse it.

2. When I cut my background fabric squares to size, I seal their edges with Fray Check to prevent raveling and distortion. This prevents me from having to overcut the block and then trim it down after stitching.

3. Fold your background fabric square in half vertically and horizontally, finger-pressing the folds. Then fold on both diagonals and finger-press. These fold lines will serve as a guide for placing the appliqué shapes on the background fabric.

4. Iron the paper templates, shiny side down, to the right side of the fabric. Using a chalk pencil (I prefer Generals brand as they mark easily), trace around the template. Make sure the line is clearly visible as this will be your turn line. Add a ⅛" – ¼" seam allowance around the template, then cut it out.

5. Pin or baste the appliqué shape in place on the background fabric square. I like Clover appliqué pins as they have a thick shaft that keeps them from backing out of the piece. Their oval heads are also less likely to snag your thread.

6. Sew the appliqué shapes in the order that they are layered, starting with the bottom pieces. Use the tip of your needle or a toothpick to turn under your seam allowance.

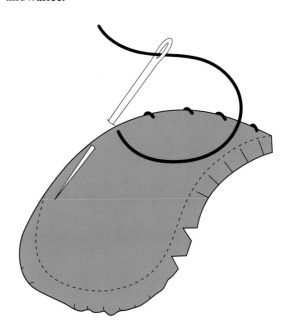

7. When appliquéing, I recommend using YLI 100-weight silk thread in a neutral color because it sinks into the fabric and practically disappears. Using a neutral color also means you won't have to worry about matching all the pieces with coordinating thread colors. YLI #242 and #235 will match any color you need.

WOOL APPLIQUÉ

I love the texture of wool appliqué. In addition to working with wool on wool, I like to mix wool with cotton backgrounds. One of the benefits of using wool is that it does not unravel, which means you do not have to turn under its edges or add a seam allowance. The process is so fast and rewarding that you will be addicted to wool appliqué after your first project!

1. Trace your templates onto the dull side of a piece of freezer paper. Cut them out on the drawn line.

2. Iron the shiny side of the templates to the wool and cut them out without a seam allowance.

3. Pin or baste the wool in place on your fabric background square.

4. To stitch, I like to use two strands of embroidery floss that will match my appliqué piece. I prefer Weeks Dye Works hand-dyed floss because it is variegated and usually best matches the hand-dyed wools I like to use. I am also in love with Simply Wool thread from The Gentle Art, Inc. This wool thread is also hand-dyed. I use one strand to appliqué. To secure the appliqué pieces, I take a ⅛" stitch perpendicular to the edge of the appliqué piece. This small, simple stitch will be barely noticeable.

SPRING

"Every spring is the only spring—a perpetual astonishment."

–Ellis Peters

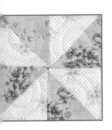

APRIL SHOWERS

Here in the Midwest, our springs are marked by rain showers and windy days. It's almost like Mother Nature is chasing the last of winter out of the way. I wanted to express that feeling in a quilt, so I placed the umbrellas in all different directions to look as though they were blowing in the wind. A simple block of twirling pinwheels makes a fitting companion, adding a sense of movement to the design. I think this light and airy throw-sized quilt is the perfect embodiment of spring, but its soft colors could carry through many other seasons.

Finished quilt: 66" x 66"
Finished block: 9" x 9"
Hand appliquéd and machine pieced by Dawn Heese
Machine quilted by Tammy Bush of Form and Function Quilting

Fabric Requirements

Block backgrounds and outer border:
4 yards cream print

Umbrella handles and tops and inner border:
1½ yards brown print

Pinwheels and umbrellas:
1¾ yards total of assorted pink, blue, red, and
   brown prints

Fray Check

Cutting Instructions

From cream print, cut:
- 7—5½" strips the width of fabric for outer border. Cut,
  then piece strips to make 2—5½" x 56½" outer border
  strips and 2—5½" x 66½" outer border strips
- 18—9½" squares. Then seal the edges with Fray Check
- 72—3½" squares
- 180—2⅜" squares

From brown print, cut:
- 6—1½" strips the width of fabric for inner border. Cut,
  then piece strips to make 2—1½" x 54½" inner border
  strips and 2—1½" x 56½" inner border strips
- 18 umbrella handle top templates on page 18
- 18 umbrella handle templates on page 18

From assorted pink, blue, red, and brown prints, cut:
- 18 umbrella templates on page 18
- 18 umbrella accent piece templates on page 18
- 180—2⅜" squares

Sewing Instructions
Appliqué Blocks

Referring to the photo for placement, appliqué the
umbrella shapes to the 9½" cream print background fabric
blocks. Please note that the top of the umbrella accent
piece is placed slightly to the right of the top center of the
umbrella piece below it. Make a total of 18 blocks.

Pinwheel Blocks

1. On the wrong side of 180—2⅜" cream print squares, draw a line from corner to corner on the diagonal.

2. With right sides together, layer a marked cream print 2⅜" square on top of a colored print 2⅜" square. Sew a ¼" seam on both sides of the drawn line. Cut apart on the drawn line and press open to yield two half-square triangle units. Repeat to make a total of 360 half-square triangle units. The units should measure 2" unfinished.

3. Join four half-square triangle units to create a pinwheel unit. Repeat to make a total of 90 pinwheel units.

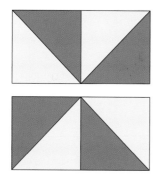

4. Referring to the diagram below, join five pinwheel units and 4—3½" cream print squares to create a pinwheel block. Repeat to make a total of 18 blocks.

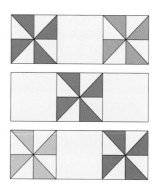

Quilt Center

1. Referring to the assembly diagram on page 17, lay out the pinwheel blocks and umbrella blocks in six rows, alternating the pinwheel and umbrella blocks.

2. Sew together blocks in each row.

3. Join rows to complete the quilt center.

Inner Border

1. Sew the 2—1½" x 54½" inner border strips to the sides of the quilt center.

2. Sew the 2—1½" x 56½" inner border strips to the top and bottom of the quilt top.

Outer Border

1. Sew the 2—5½" x 56½" outer border strips to the sides of the quilt top.

2. Sew the 2—5½" x 66½" outer border strips to the top and bottom of the quilt top.

Layer quilt top, batting, and backing. Baste, then quilt as desired.

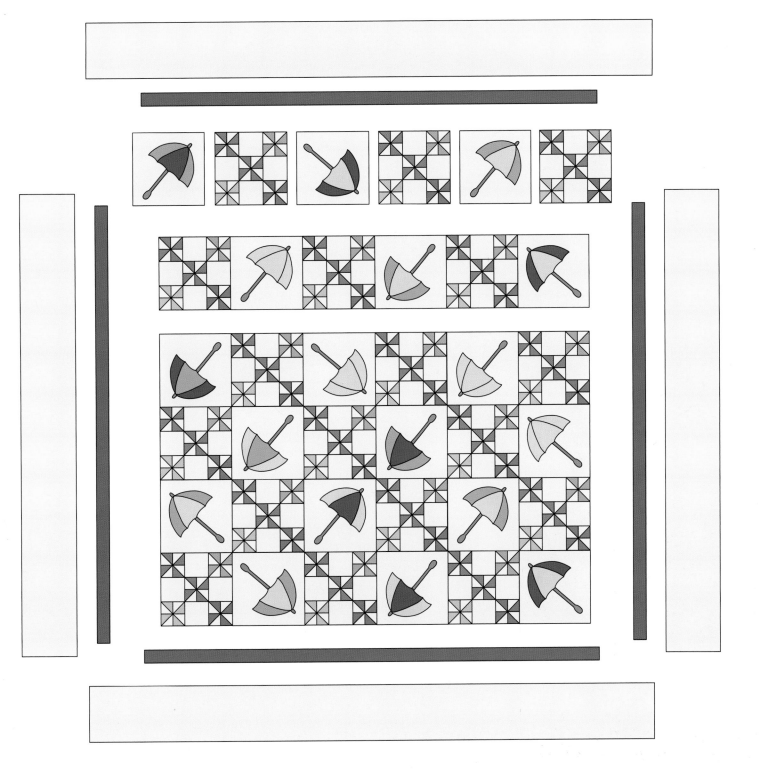

ASSEMBLY DIAGRAM

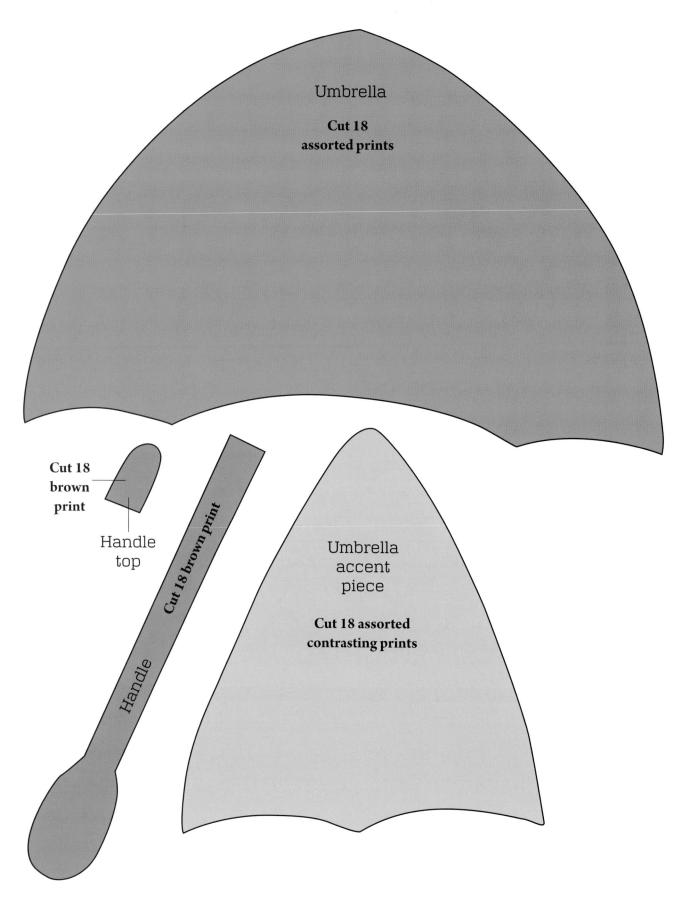

Umbrella

**Cut 18
assorted prints**

**Cut 18
brown
print**

Handle
top

Cut 18 brown print

Handle

Umbrella
accent
piece

**Cut 18 assorted
contrasting prints**

Templates do NOT include a seam allowance

BUFFALO CHECK PILLOW

Accent pillows are a fast and easy way to change the mood of a room. I have a closet full of little pillows that I toss on the couch, bed, or even in boxes to change the feel of my décor. Made with a simple dish towel like the kind you can find in many quilt shops, this pillow is especially quick to make. With minimal sewing and some quick wool appliqué, you can have it completed in practically no time.

Material Requirements

1 dish towel
8—2½" x 6" assorted colored wool scraps
4" x 6" brown wool scrap
Polyester fiberfill
6—1"-wide buttons

Cutting Instructions

From assorted wool scraps, cut:
• 2 each of the four umbrella segment templates below

From brown wool scrap, cut:
• 2 umbrella handle templates below
• 2 umbrella handle top templates below

Because felted wool does not fray, there is no need to turn under the edges. Do not add a seam allowance to the template pieces listed below.

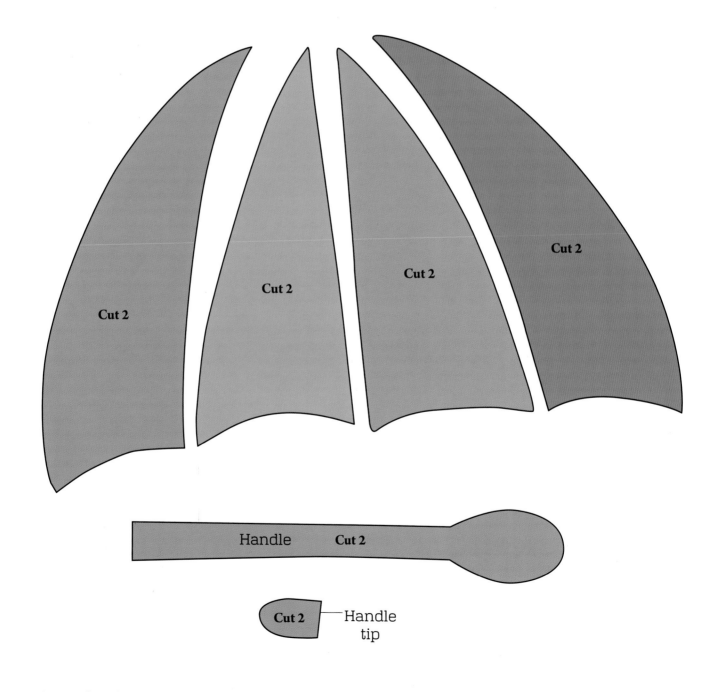

Cut 2

Cut 2

Cut 2

Cut 2

Handle   Cut 2

Cut 2 — Handle tip

Hand appliquéd by Dawn Heese
Approximate finished size: 10˝ x 28˝

Sewing Instructions

1. With wrong sides together, fold the towel in half lengthwise. Find and mark the center of this area.

2. Referring to the photo above for placement, center and sew the appliqué shapes on the towel. There should be about 3 inches between the two umbrellas.

3. With wrong sides together, sew a ½" seam along the top and bottom of the towel, creating a topstitch effect.

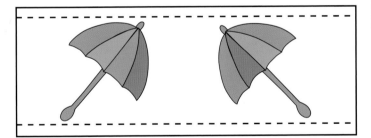

4. Measure 4 inches from each end of the towel and mark. Sew a seam along this marked line to create a flange for the pillow. Sew along the other end, leaving an opening for stuffing.

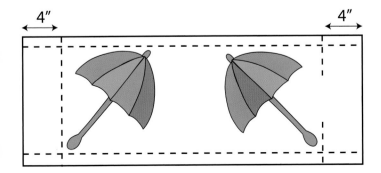

4˝   4˝

5. Stuff the pillow tightly with polyester fiberfill and whipstitch the opening closed. Sew three buttons on each flange end.

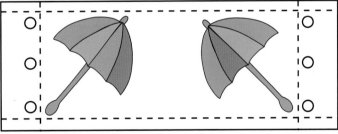

No-Bake Cheesecake

I love all kinds of cheesecake. I make several kinds, but in the spring, I enjoy making this no-bake recipe with Cool Whip. I hope you will love it as much as my family and I do!

- 2—8 oz. packages of cream cheese packages at room temperature
- 8 oz. package of Cool Whip
- 8 oz. container of sour cream
- ½ cup sugar
- 1 teaspoon vanilla
- ½ teaspoon lemon juice
- 1 large or 2 small ready-made graham cracker pie crusts
- 1 can cherry pie filling

Blend together the cream cheese, sour cream, sugar, vanilla, and lemon juice in a mixer until smooth. Add Cool Whip and mix until well blended. Pour mixture into pie crusts. Refrigerate. Then top with pie filling before serving.

SUMMER

"Deep summer is when laziness finds respectability."

–Sam Keen

SASSY

As summer arrives, I spend more time outside tending to my flowers and gardens. I still like to quilt but my projects tend to be smaller or ones that come together more quickly. Large appliqué pieces and easy piecing make speedy work of this quilted throw.

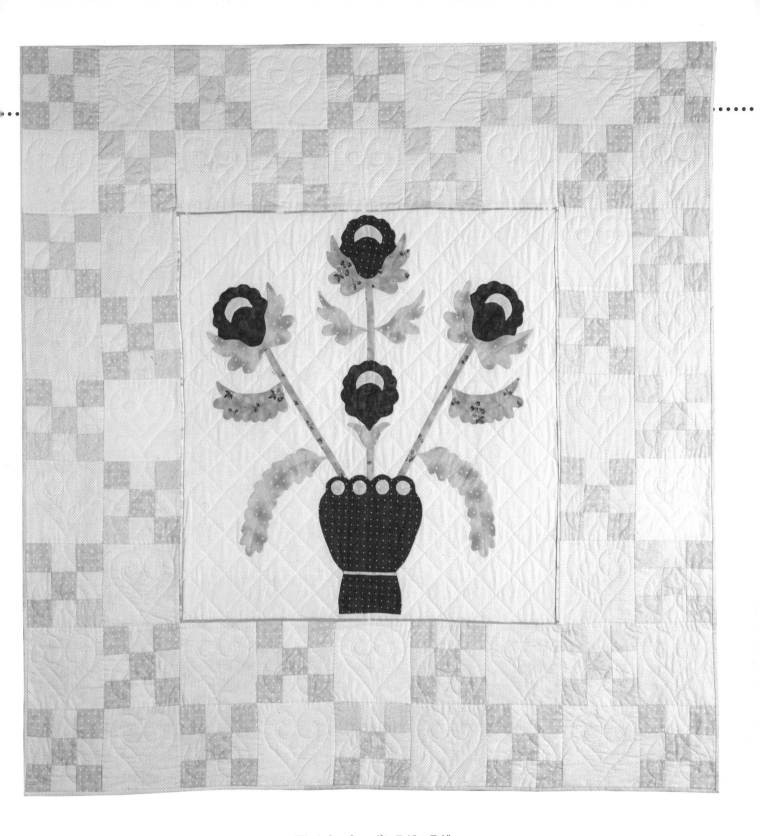

Finished quilt: 54" x 54"
Finished appliqué block: 30" x 30"
Finished pieced block: 6" x 6"
Hand appliquéd, machine pieced, and hand-quilted by Dawn Heese

Fabric Requirements

Nine-Patch blocks:

1 yard total of assorted pale blue prints (this also covers the yardage needed for the appliqué blocks below)

Appliqué block backgrounds, Nine-Patch block backgrounds, and setting squares:

2½ yard total of assorted cream dots
Blue print yardage listed in previous heading

Appliqué block:

½ yard total of assorted green prints
⅓ yard total of assorted red prints

3½ yards blue ¾"-wide double-sided ribbon
   (I used Ribbon FX from Hobby Lobby)
Fray Check
¼" and ½" bias tape makers

Cutting Instructions

From assorted pale blue prints, cut:
- 10—2½" x 30" strips for Nine-Patch blocks
- 2—2½" x 35" strips for Nine-Patch blocks
- 4 circle templates on page 31
- 4 flower accents on page 32
- 1 decorative band approximately 5" long near vase base after making it with a ¼" bias tape maker

From assorted cream dots, cut:
- 1—30" x 30" square for appliqué background. Then seal edges with Fray Check
- 28—6½" squares for setting squares
- 5—2½" x 30" strips for Nine-Patch blocks
- 4—2½" x 35" strips for Nine-Patch blocks

From assorted red prints, cut:
- 1 vase template on page 31
- 4 flower templates on page 32

From assorted green prints, cut:
- 1 Leaf A template on page 31
- 2 Leaf B templates on page 31
- 3 Leaf C templates on page 32
- 2 Leaf D templates 33
- 2 Leaf E templates on page 33
- 3 stems after making them with a ½" bias tape maker

From ribbon, cut:
- 4—30½"-long pieces

Sewing Instructions

Appliqué Blocks

Referring to the diagram below for placement, sew the appliqué pieces to the 30" cream dot background square.

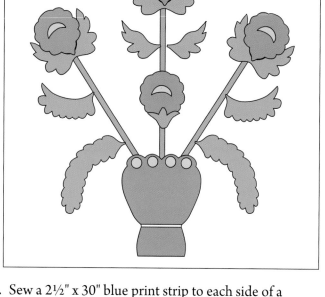

1. Sew a 2½" x 30" blue print strip to each side of a 2½" x 30" cream dot strip. Repeat to make a total of five strip sets.

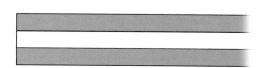

2. Cut the strip from Step 1 into 2½" x 6½" subsets to yield a total of 56 sets.

3. Sew a 2½ "x 35" cream dot strip to each side of a 2½" x 35" blue print strip. Repeat to make a total of two strip sets.

4. Cut the strip from Step 3 into 2½" x 6½" subsets to yield a total of 28 sets.

5. Sew two strips from Step 2 to one strip from Step 4 to create a Nine-Patch block. Repeat to make a total of 28 Nine-Patch blocks.

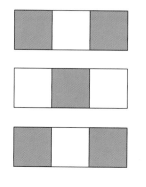
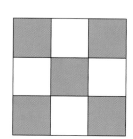

Quilt Center

1. Fold the ribbon in half lengthwise. Then align the un-folded edge with the raw edge of the appliqué block.

2. Using a scant ¼" seam allowance, sew the ribbon to the sides of the block. Repeat for the top and bottom of the block.

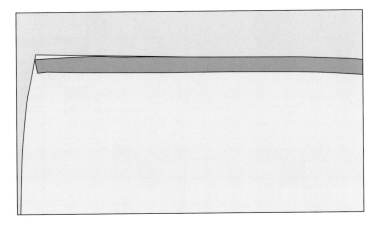

3. Referring to the assembly diagram on page 30, lay out the 28 Nine-Patch blocks and 28—9½" setting squares.

4. Referring to the assembly diagram, sew the Nine-Patch blocks and setting blocks into rows.

5. Sew the central appliqué block to the two sections comprised of five Nine-Patch blocks and five setting blocks.

6. Join the rows to complete the quilt top.

Layer quilt top, batting, and backing. Baste, then quilt as desired.

ASSEMBLY DIAGRAM

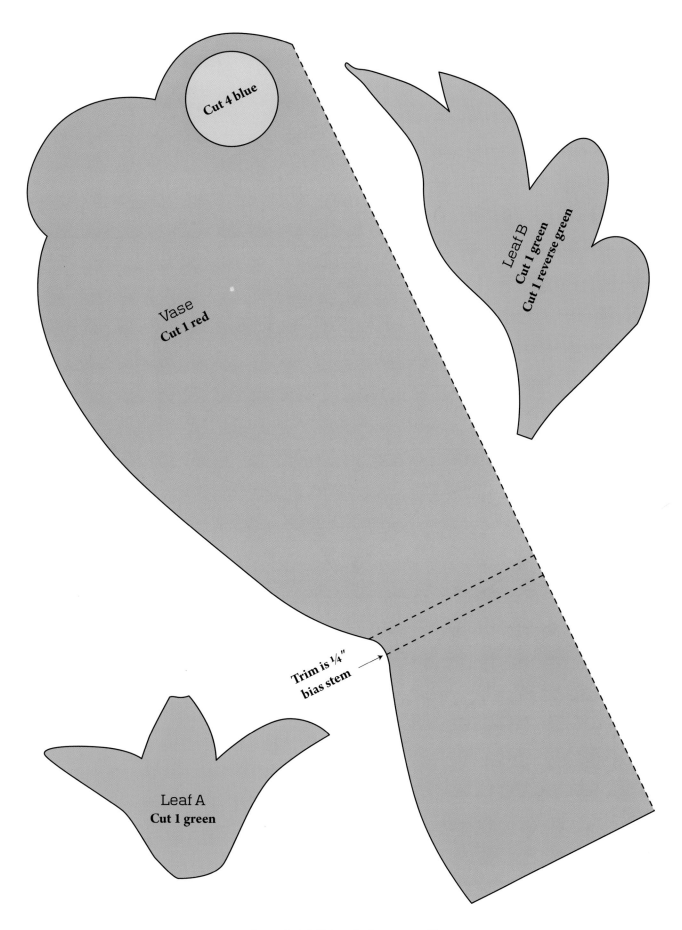

Cut 4 blue

Vase
Cut 1 red

Leaf B
**Cut 1 green
Cut 1 reverse green**

**Trim is ¼"
bias stem**

Leaf A
Cut 1 green

Templates do NOT include a seam allowance

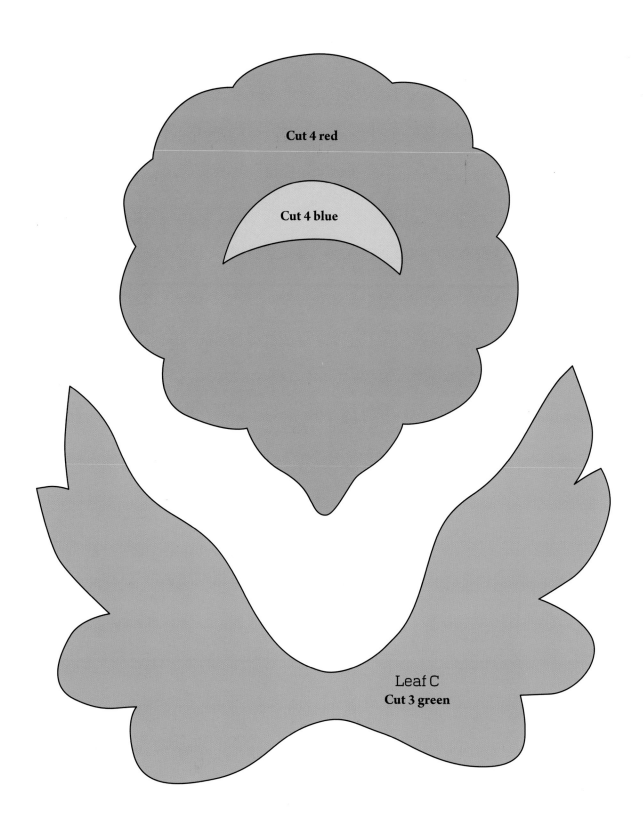

Cut 4 red

Cut 4 blue

Leaf C
Cut 3 green

Templates do NOT include a seam allowance

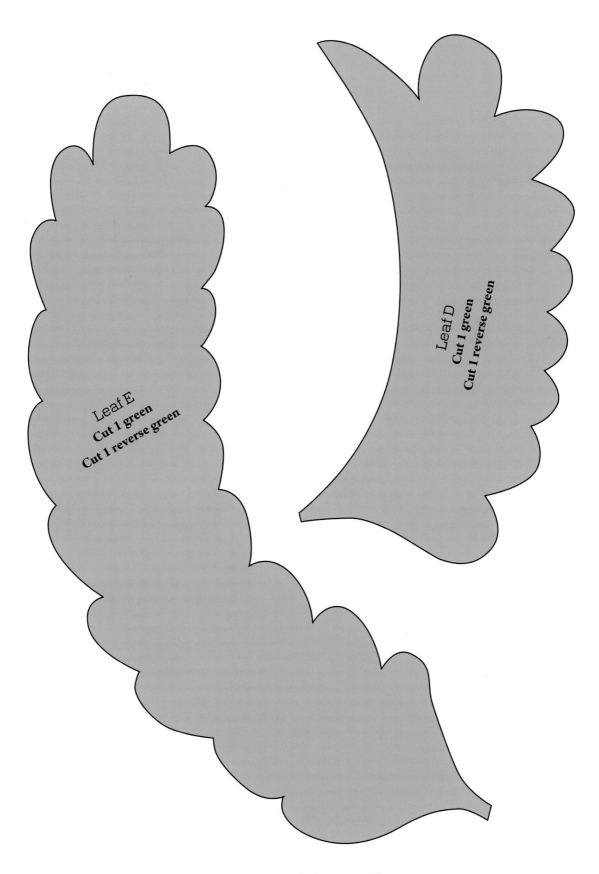

Leaf E
Cut 1 green
Cut 1 reverse green

Leaf D
Cut 1 green
Cut 1 reverse green

Templates do NOT include a seam allowance

CROSS STITCH PINKEEP

I love counted cross stitch and the old look of this piece. Because it's small, this pinkeep is the perfect project to work on while on the go. Once you're finished, simply fill it with pins and keep it handy by your sewing area—or set it on a shelf for a charming seasonal display.

Finished pinkeep: 3½" x 7¾"
Stitched by Dawn Heese

Material Requirements

6" x 7½" piece of Zweigart 28-ct. cashel Summer
  Khaki linen
5" x 13" red print
Weeks Dye Works embroidery floss:
  Aqua (2131), Sage (1246), Hibiscus (2278),
  and Grapefruit (2245)
5"-long piece of trim
1 button
Polyester fiberfill

Cutting Instructions

From red print, cut:
- 1—3¼" x 4" rectangle
- 1—4" x 8¼" rectangle

From trim, cut:
- 1—4" long piece

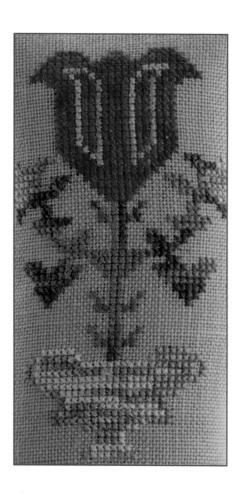

Finishing Instructions

1. Referring to the floss key on page 37, stitch the design on page 37.

2. Trim the stitched piece to measure 4" x 5½".

3. Using a ¼" seam allowance, sew the 3¼" x 4" red print rectangle to the bottom of the trimmed stitched piece. Press the seam toward the red print.

4. Align the edge of the trim with the seam line where you joined the stitched piece to the red print. Sew it in place.

5. Referring to the photo on page 35 for placement, stitch a button on top of the trim 1" from the left edge.

6. With right sides together, layer the pinkeep front on top of the 4" x 8¼" red print rectangle. Using a ¼" seam allowance, sew around the perimeter, leaving a small opening to turn the pinkeep right side out.

7. Turn the pinkeep right side out and stuff it with polyester fiberfill. Then whipstitch the opening closed.

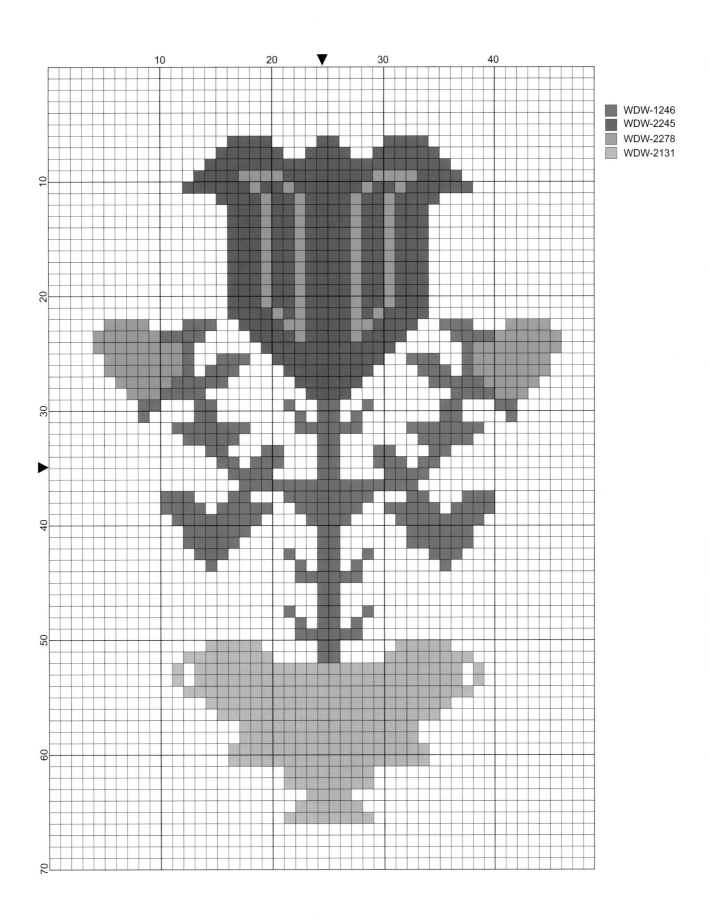

WDW-1246
WDW-2245
WDW-2278
WDW-2131

Tortellini Salad

Our summers here in Missouri are hot, so I try not to use the oven any more than I have to. This cold dish makes a delicious supper for summer evenings.

- 6 oz. bag frozen cheese tortellini
- 6 oz. bag frozen beef tortellini
- 2 fresh tomatoes
- 3 green onions
- ⅓ cup parsley
- ½ cup black olives
- ¾ cup parmesan peppercorn ranch dressing

Cook the tortellini according to directions on the bag. Rinse with cold water. Chop the tomatoes, onion, and parsley. Add them to the pasta, then add the black olives and dressing. Mix well. Refrigerate for an hour.

AUTUMN

"*Autumn is a second spring when every leaf is in flower.*"
–Albert Camus

PUMPKIN BLOSSOMS

Fall is my favorite time of year. The mornings have a bit of chill but the days are comfortable. In my area, we have a wide variety of trees that turn many different shades in the fall. Inspired by their color palette, this quilt features shades of rust and orange with just a pop of purple. It is generously sized for snuggling under on those cool autumn evenings.

Finished quilt: 70" x 70"
Finished block: 18" x 18"
Hand appliquéd and machine pieced by Dawn Heese
Machine quilted by Tammy Bush of Form and Function Quilting

Fabric Requirements

Block and border backgrounds:
4¾ yards total of assorted tan prints

Block and border appliqué:
1¾ yards total of assorted green prints
4 yards total of assorted orange, gold, rust, and
    red prints
¾ yard total of assorted purple prints

Fray Check
¾" bias tape marker

Cutting Instructions

From assorted tan prints, cut:
• 9—18½" squares. Then seal the edges with Fray Check
• 16—8½" x 14" rectangles for the border swag
    backgrounds. Then seal the edges with Fray Check
• 4—8½" x 8½" squares for the border corner swag
    backgrounds. Then seal the edges with Fray Check

From assorted green prints, cut:
• 72 leaf templates on page 46
• 36 pumpkin blossom leaf templates on page 46
• 18 stems with a ¾" bias tape maker
• 24 circle templates on page 47

**From assorted orange, gold, rust, red, and purple
prints, cut:**
• 36 pumpkin blossom templates on page 46
• 16 swag templates on page 47
• 4 corner swag templates on page 47

Sewing Instructions

Bloom Blocks
Referring to the photo on page 43 for placement, sew the appliqué shapes to the 18½" assorted tan print square background blocks. Repeat to make a total of nine blocks.

Swag Blocks
Referring to the photo below for placement, sew the swag appliqué shapes to the 8½" x 14" assorted tan print background blocks. Repeat to make a total of 16 swag blocks.

Corner Swag Blocks
Referring to the photo below for placement, sew the corner swag appliqué shapes to the 8½" square assorted tan print background blocks. Repeat to make a total of four corner swag blocks.

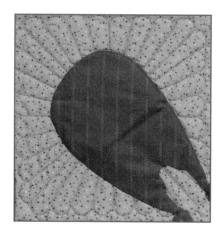

Quilt Center

1. Lay out the nine appliqué blocks. Then sew the bloom blocks in three rows of three blocks each to create the quilt center.

2. Appliqué a circle template on page 47 at the intersection of the seams.

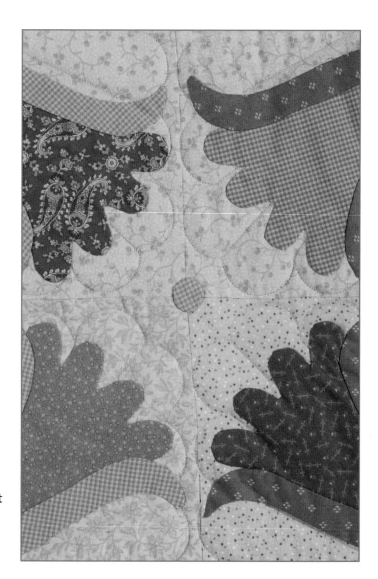

Pumpkin Blossoms Block	Pumpkin Blossoms Block	Pumpkin Blossoms Block
Pumpkin Blossoms Block	Pumpkin Blossoms Block	Pumpkin Blossoms Block
Pumpkin Blossoms Block	Pumpkin Blossoms Block	Pumpkin Blossoms Block

Border

1. Join four swag blocks to make a side border strip. Repeat to make a total of two side border strips.

2. Appliqué a green circle template on page 47 at the intersections of the swag blocks.

3. Referring to the assembly diagram on page 45, sew the two border strips from Step 2 to the sides of the quilt center.

4. Join four swag blocks with two corner blocks to make a top border strip. Repeat to make one for the bottom border strip. Then appliqué a circle where each of the swags meet.

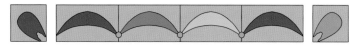

5. Sew the two strips to the top and bottom of the quilt top. Then appliqué a green circle where the corner swags meet the side border swags.

Layer quilt top, batting, and backing. Baste, then quilt as desired.

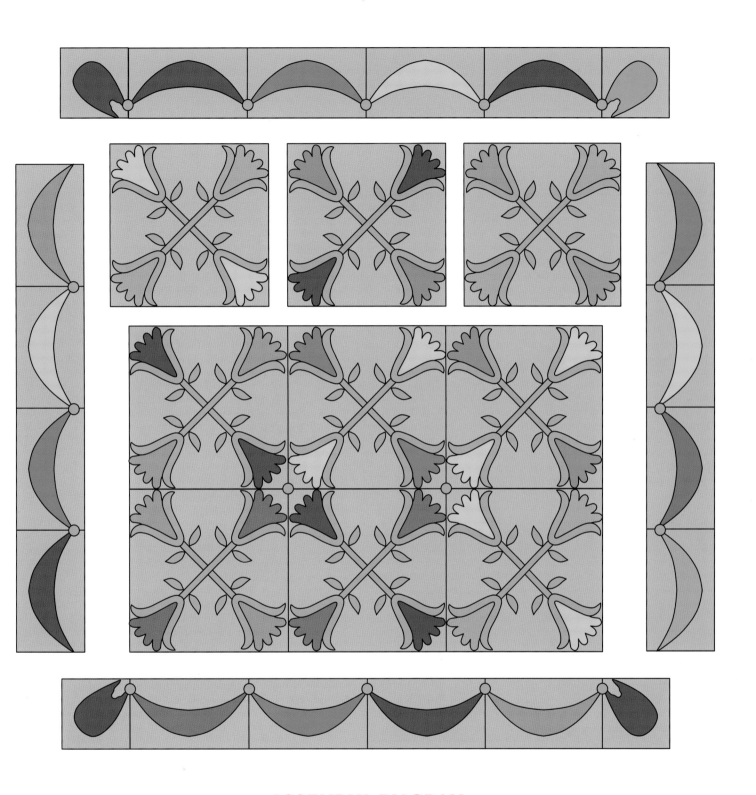

ASSEMBLY DIAGRAM

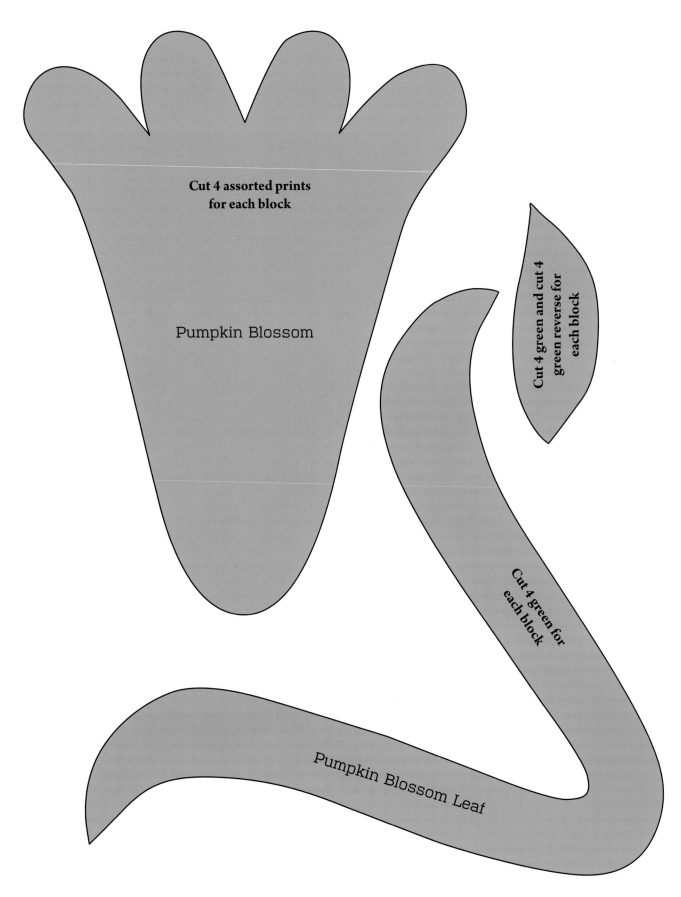

**Cut 4 assorted prints
for each block**

Pumpkin Blossom

Cut 4 green and cut 4
green reverse for
each block

Cut 4 green for
each block

Pumpkin Blossom Leaf

Templates do NOT include a seam allowance

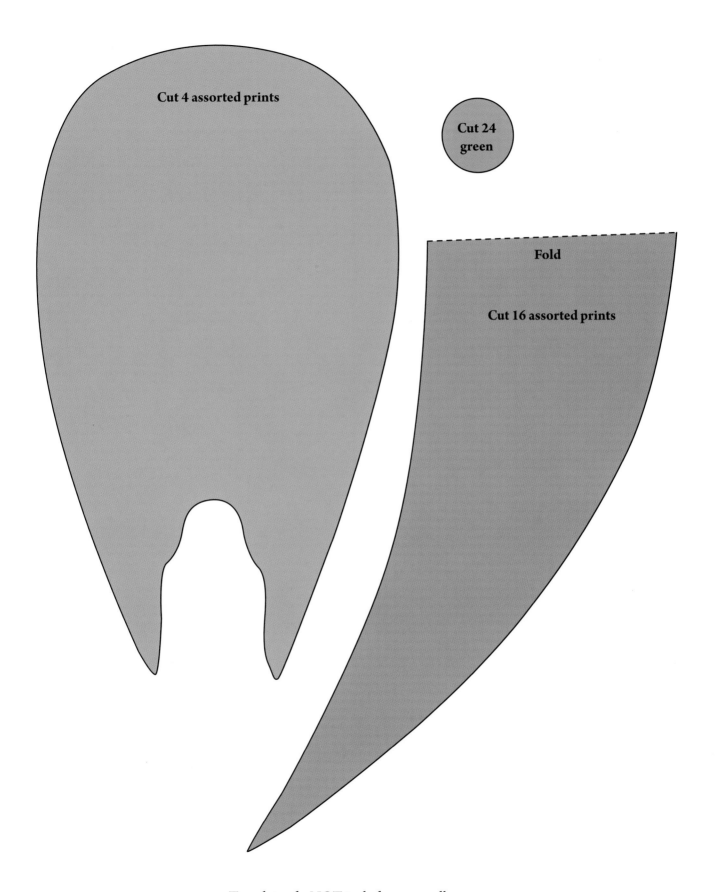

Cut 4 assorted prints

Cut 24 green

Fold

Cut 16 assorted prints

Templates do NOT include a seam allowance

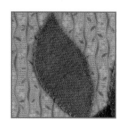

PUMPKIN BLOSSOMS PILLOW

The perfect fabrics for fall, wool and flannel make this comfy pillow a welcome addition to any room.

Fabric Requirements

1 fat eighth orange wool
1 fat eighth purple wool
1 fat eighth green wool
⅝ cream flannel
2½ yards purple braid trim

Fray Check

Cutting Instructions

Because felted wool does not fray, there is no need to turn under the edges.

From orange wool, cut:
• 2 pumpkin blossom templates on page 46

From purple wool, cut:
• 2 pumpkin blossom templates on page 46

From green wool, cut:
• 8 leaf templates on page 46
• 4 pumpkin blossom leaf templates on page 46
• 2—¾"-wide strips for stems

From flannel, cut:
• 2—18½" squares. Then seal the edges of one with Fray Check

Finished pillow: 18" x 18"
Hand appliquéd and machine sewn by Dawn Heese

Sewing Instructions

1. Referring to the photo above for placement, sew the appliqué pieces to the 18½" flannel background square.

2. With right sides together and using a ¼" seam allowance, sew the appliqué block to the remaining 18½" flannel square, leaving an opening at the bottom for turning the pillow right side out.

3. Turn the pillow right side out.

4. Stuff the pillow with polyester fiberfill.

5. Tuck one end of the purple braid in the opening you left for turning the pillow right side out. Then cover the seam by sewing the braid around the pillow with a small hidden stitch by hand. Tuck the end of the braid in the opening and stitch the pillow closed.

Apple Crisp

I love the smell of pies baking but don't always have the time to make them. This is a delicious alternative.

- 2 cans apple pie filling
- 1 box yellow cake mix
- 1 stick real butter

Pre-heat oven to 375 degrees. Pour the two cans of apple pie filling into a 9" x 13" pan. Sprinkle the yellow cake mix evenly over the top. Dice the butter in small pieces and scatter over the top of the cake mix. Bake for 45 minutes or until golden brown. Serve the pie warm, topped with whipped topping or ice cream.

WINTER

"Winter is the time for comfort, for good food and warmth, for the touch of a friendly hand and for a talk beside the fire; it is the time for home."
–Edith Sitwell

WINTER BLUES

When I think of winter, I seem to think in terms of blues. For this quilt, I wanted to convey the coolness of that season while creating a project that could be used long after it was over. I love stars, which dance and twinkle across this quilt. And in the spirit of winter, they could be interpreted as snowflakes of a sort.

Finished quilt: 66" x 78"
Finished block: 12" x 12"
Machine pieced by Dawn Heese
Machine quilted by Tammy Bush of Form and Function Quilting

Fabric Requirements

Block backgrounds and outer border:
4⅛ yards total of assorted off-white prints

Stars and inner border:
3⅛ yards total of assorted blue prints

Cutting Instructions

From assorted off-white prints, cut:

- 60—3½" squares
- 60—3⅞" squares
- 300—1½" squares
- 300—1⅞" squares
- 60—4½" squares
- 4—2½" strips the width of fabric for outer border. Join two strips end to end, then cut to measure 2½" x 74½". Repeat to make a total of two strips
- 4—2½" strips the width of fabric for outer border. Join two strips end to end, then cut to measure 2½" x 66½". Repeat to make a total of two strips

From assorted blue prints, cut:

- 60—3⅞" squares
- 15—6½" squares
- 300—1⅞" squares
- 75—2½" squares
- Random lengths of 1½"-wide strips for inner border (For a scrappy look, Dawn used assorted blue prints rather than just one). Then join strips end to end to measure 72½". Repeat to make a total of two strips
- Random lengths of 1½"-wide strips for inner border (For a scrappy look, Dawn used assorted blue prints rather than just one). Then join strips end to end to measure 62½". Repeat to make a total of two strips

Sewing Instructions

Large Star Blocks

1. On the wrong side of the 60 off-white 3⅞" squares, draw a diagonal line from corner to corner.

2. With right sides together, layer a marked 3⅞" off-white square on top of a 3⅞" blue square. Sew a ¼" seam on both sides of the line. Then cut apart on the drawn line and press open to yield two half-square triangle units. Repeat to make a total of 120 half-square triangle units.

3. Sew two half-square triangle units from Step 2 to 2—3½" squares to create a row. Repeat to make a total of 30 rows.

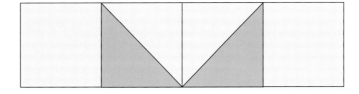

4. Sew two half-square triangle units to each side of a 6½" blue square. Repeat to make a total of 15 units.

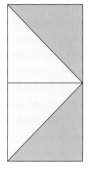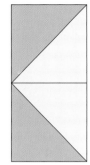

5. Sew two rows from Step 3 to the unit from Step 4 to create a star block. Repeat to make a total of 15 blocks.

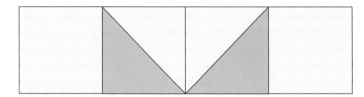

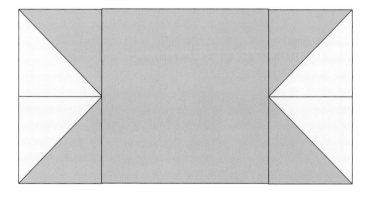

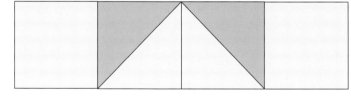

Five-Star Blocks

1. On the wrong side of the 300—1⅞" off-white squares, draw a diagonal line from corner to corner.

2. With right sides together, layer a marked off-white 1⅞" square on top of a blue 1⅞" square. Sew a ¼" seam on both sides of the drawn line. Then cut apart on the drawn line and press open to yield two half-square triangle units. Repeat to make a total of 600 half-square triangles units.

3. Sew two half-square triangle units from Step 2 to 2—1½" off-white squares to create a row. Repeat to make a total of 150 rows.

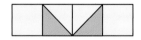

4. Sew two half-square triangle units to each side of a 2½" blue print square. Repeat to make a total of 75 units.

5. Sew two rows from Step 3 to the unit from Step 4 to create a star block. Repeat to make a total of 75 blocks.

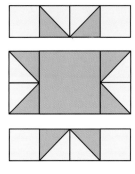

6. Join 5 star blocks with 4—4½" off-white squares to complete the block. Repeat to create a total of 15 blocks.

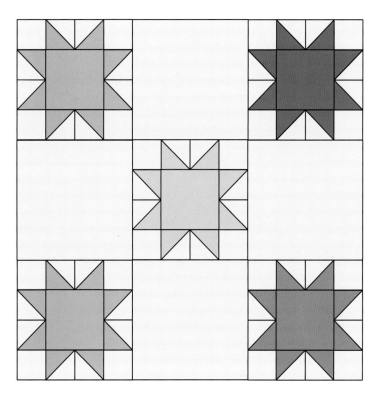

Quilt Center

Referring to the assembly diagram on page 57, lay out the 15 Five-Star blocks and 15 single star blocks. Assemble the blocks in rows, then join rows, to complete the quilt center.

Inner Border

1. Referring to the assembly diagram on page 57, sew the 2—1½" x 72½" blue print strips to the sides of the quilt center.

2. Sew the 2—1½" x 62½" blue print strips to the top and bottom of the quilt top.

Outer Border

1. Referring to the assembly diagram, sew the 2—2½" x 74½" off-white print strips to the sides of the quilt top.

2. Sew the 2—2½" x 66½" strips to the top and bottom of the quilt top.

Layer quilt top, batting, and backing. Baste, then quilt as desired.

ASSEMBLY DIAGRAM

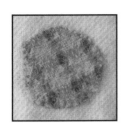

WINTER BLUES TABLE MAT

I found some gorgeous hand-dyed wool in the Primitive Gatherings booth at Quilt Market last year and knew I had to have it. They made this cozy table mat—the perfect complement to my Winter Blues quilt.

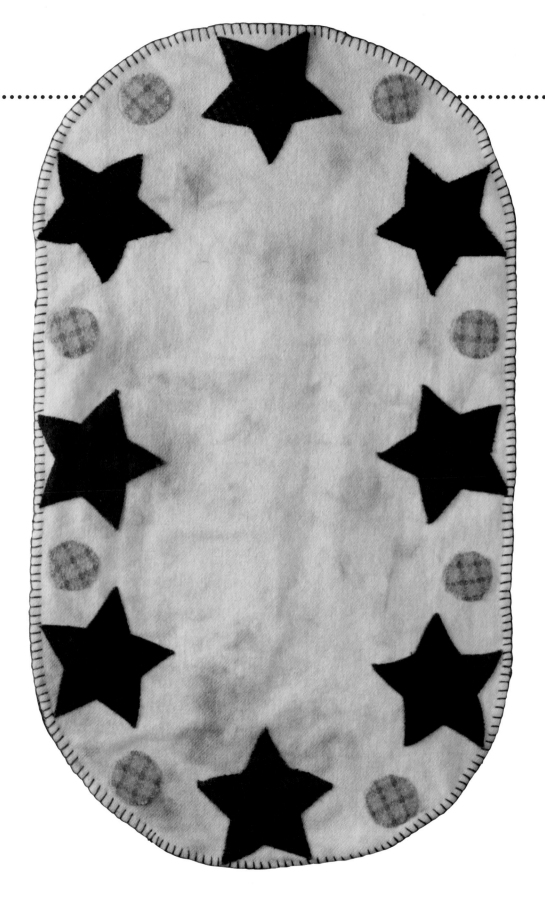

Finished mat: 13" x 24"
Hand appliquéd by Dawn Heese

Fabric Requirements

Appliqué background:
½ yard off-white wool

Backing:
½ yard blue print fabric

Appliqué:
Fat quarter blue wool
Fat eighth gold wool

Blue No. 8 perle cotton

Cutting Instructions

Because felted wool does not fray, there is no need to turn under the edges.

From off-white wool, cut:
• 1 oval background template on pages 61-63 (Be sure to add a ¼" seam allowance to the template before cutting)

From blue print fabric, cut:
• 1 oval background template on pages 61-63 (Be sure to add a ¼" seam allowance to the template before cutting)

From blue wool, cut:
• 8 star templates on page 62

From gold wool, cut:
• 8 circle templates on page 62

Sewing Instructions

1. Referring to the following diagram for placement, appliqué the wool shapes onto the off-white wool background.

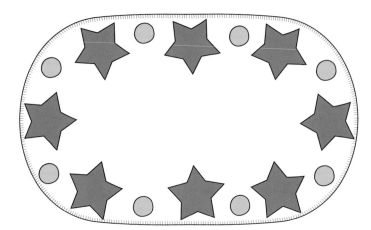

2. With right sides together, layer the finished off-white wool appliquéd oval from Step 1 on top of the blue print fabric oval. Then sew around the perimeter with a ¼" seam allowance, leaving an opening for turning the table mat right side out.

3. Turn the table mat right side out, then press.

4. Whipstitch the opening closed.

5. Using the blue perle cotton, sew a buttonhole stitch around the mat's entire perimeter.

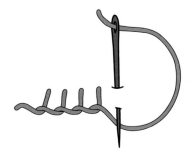

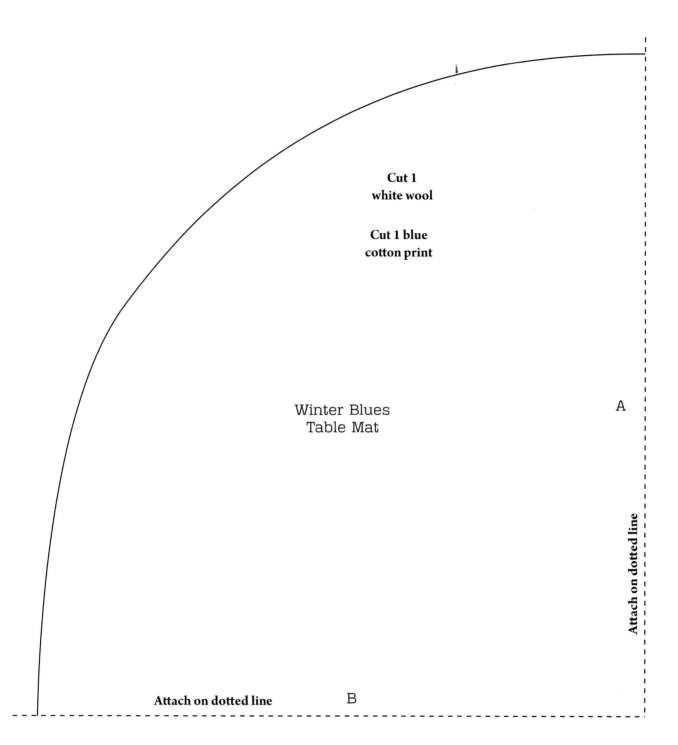

**Cut 1
white wool**

**Cut 1 blue
cotton print**

Winter Blues
Table Mat

A

Attach on dotted line

Attach on dotted line   B

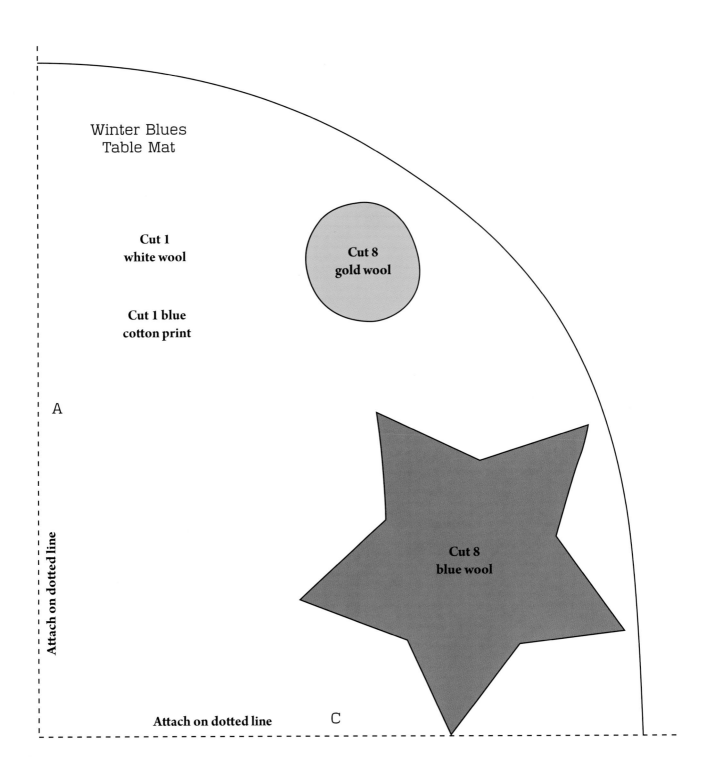

Winter Blues
Table Mat

Cut 1
white wool

Cut 1 blue
cotton print

Cut 8
gold wool

A

Attach on dotted line

Cut 8
blue wool

Attach on dotted line   C

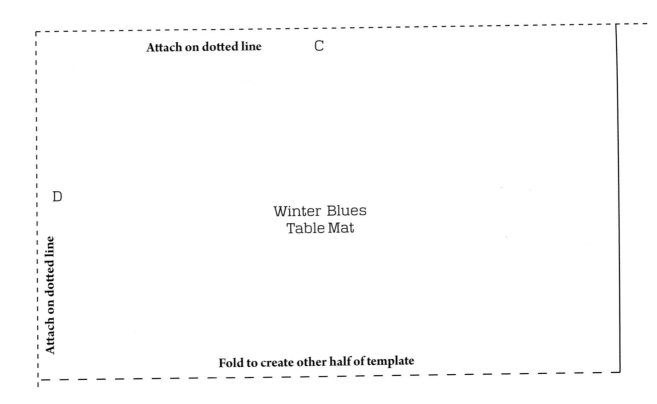

Attach on dotted line B

Attach on dotted line

D

Winter Blues
Table Mat

Fold to create other half of template

Attach on dotted line C

D

Attach on dotted line

Winter Blues
Table Mat

Fold to create other half of template

Taco Soup

What better dish to indulge in during winter than a warm bowl of soup? At my house, we love soup and this recipe is an all-time family favorite.

- 1 lb. ground beef
- 2 cans black beans, undrained
- 1 can corn, undrained
- 28 oz. can diced tomatoes
- 1 package Hidden Valley Fiesta Ranch dressing mix
- 1 package Chi Chi's taco seasoning
- 1 cup water
- 1 medium onion, chopped

In a dutch oven, brown the ground beef and onion. Add remaining ingredients, mix well, and bring to a boil. Reduce heat and let simmer for 20 minutes. Garnish with cheese and corn chips.